C000280700

Lake District

Compiled by
Terry Marsh

JARROLD

Mapping sourced from Ordnance Survey®

Text: Terry Marsh
Photography: Terry Marsh, Bill Birkett, John Curtis, Audrey Marsh, Charles Nicholas
Editorial: Ark Creative (UK) Ltd
Design: Ark Creative (UK) Ltd

© Jarrold 2008, a trading division of Pitkin Publishing

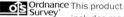
Jarrold
ISBN: 978-0-7117-5004-3

While every care has been taken to ensure the accuracy of the route directions, the publishers cannot accept responsibility for errors or omissions, or for changes in details given. The countryside is not static: hedges and fences can be removed, field boundaries can alter, footpaths can be rerouted and changes in ownership can result in the closure or diversion of some concessionary paths. Also, paths that are easy and pleasant for walking in fine conditions may become slippery, muddy and difficult in wet weather, while stepping stones across rivers and streams may become impassable.

If you find an inaccuracy in either the text or maps, please write to or e-mail Jarrold at the addresses below.

First published 2001
Revised and reprinted 2004, 2005, 2008.

Printed in Singapore. 5/08

Pitkin Publishing
Healey House, Dene Road, Andover, Hampshire SP10 2AA
email: info@totalwalking.co.uk
www.totalwalking.co.uk

Front cover: Alamy (Leslie Garland Picture Library)
Previous page: Greendale, near Wastwater

Contents

Keymap

SCALE 1:250 000 or 1 INCH to 4 MILES *1CM to 2.5KM*

| 0 | 2 | 4 | 6 | 8 | 10 | KILOMETRES | 15 |

| 0 | 2 | 4 | 6 | MILES | 8 | 10 |

KEYMAP HEIGHTS SHOWN IN METRES

Introduction

The routes and information in this book have been devised specifically
with families and children in mind. All the walks include points of
interest as well as a question to provide an objective.

If you, or your children, have not walked before, choose from the shorter
walks for your first outings. The purpose is not simply to get from A to B
but to enjoy an exploration, which may be just a steady stroll in the
countryside.

The walks are graded by length and difficulty, but few landscapes are
truly flat, so even shorter walks may involve some ascent. Details are
given under Route Features in the first information box for each route.
But the precise nature of the ground underfoot will depend on recent
weather conditions. If you do set out on a walk and discover the going
is harder than you expected, or the weather has deteriorated, do not
be afraid to turn back. The route will always be there another day,
when you are fitter or the children are more experienced or the weather
is better.

Bear in mind that the countryside also changes. Landmarks may disappear,
gates may become styles, rights of way may be altered. However, with the
aid of this book and its maps you should be able enjoy many interesting
family walks in the countryside.

The Lake District

For walkers the thing that is so inspiring about the Lake District is the
huge choice. At one end of the scale you can enjoy a simple stroll beside a
lake, through a valley or alongside a river, at the other extreme you can
set off boldly to 'conquer' a particular summit, though there are no
unconquered summits here! Between the two ends of this spectrum are
countless permutations of possibility, enough, certainly, to last a lifetime.

There are over 2,225 miles (3,560km) of public footpaths and bridleways
in the Lake District, and many miles of permissive pathways where the

consent of the landowner enables walkers to explore where rights of way do not exist. These are the most prized recreation resource throughout the whole of the National Park and represent a chance for visitors (and residents) to enjoy the countryside

Castlerigg Stone Circle

and the unique quality of its landscape.

Initially, it was the waterfalls and 'viewing the set landscapes' that were the main reasons for people to come to the Lakes. But increasingly, guidebooks devoted more space to the surrounding summits as the pleasures of mountain walking became more popular. The earliest records of visitors walking on the mountains date from the end of the 18th century, but interest became particularly intensified during the early part of the 19th.

In 1823, Jonathan Otley, a Keswick guide, looked upon as the father of Lakeland geology, produced the wonderfully titled book, *A Concise Description of the English Lakes, The Mountains in their vicinity, And the Roads by which they may be visited; With Essays on Mineralogy and Geology, on Meteorology, the Floating Island on Derwent Lake, and the Black-Lead Mine in Borrowdale, and Map of the District*. Unlike other, purely descriptive, books of the time, Otley's was the first describing walking routes through the mountains.

During the 19th century, walking was a serious and complex affair, and climbing a Lake District mountain approached in much the same way as an Alpine summit. Ponies were used to transport equipment and refreshments, and guides were hired. But it was a quantum leap for mankind when perceptions turned 'mountains' into 'fells'. Soon it was commonplace to find many of the valleys echoing to the sound of walkers as the pursuit of fell walking took on a new dimension.

In no small measure, the advancement of fell walking during the second half of the 20th century, can be attributed to the work of Alfred Wainwright, sometime Borough Treasurer of Kendal, who, over a period of 13 years, produced his classic collection of *Pictorial Guides to the Lakeland Fells*. They are unquestionably unique and amazingly skilful works of art, although as practical guides they have been replaced by a vast and well-written selection of up-to-date books by contemporary authors.

Strangely, in spite of its name, the Lake District has only one 'lake', Bassenthwaite; all the others are 'tarns', 'meres' or 'waters', though 16 of them fall within the conventional understanding of a lake. Indeed, Windermere is England's longest lake ($10^{1/2}$ miles/17km from Waterhead to Lakeside) and Wastwater its deepest (258ft/79m).

But the lakes are only one ingredient among the many that make the landscape quality of Lakeland what it is: the fells, which, in Scafell Pike, include England's highest, the valleys or dales, and the towns and villages – almost 400 of them – all contribute to satisfy the vision of John Dower, whose report, published in 1945, augured the development of National Parks as extensive areas of 'beautiful and relatively wild country...which should be preserved for the benefit of the nation'.

Lakeland is a place of extremes, for not only does it boast the longest and deepest lakes in England and its highest mountains, but here, too, you'll find the steepest roads (Hardknott Pass is 33 per cent, or 1-in-3; Kirkstone and Honister are both 25 per cent, or 1-in-4). St Olaf's Church in Wasdale is claimed to be the smallest church in England. In Mardale, you may see England's only golden eagles and at Santon Bridge listen to the World's Biggest Liar.

But the real beauty of the Lake District is change, from the geological shifts that only time can trace and the subtle variations wrought by the rivers and streams to the fleeting essays of light that brighten the fellsides and lowland pastures and the signature of wind across the surface of a lake. It is change, and a few indefinable qualities that brings so many visitors, in all seasons and weathers, to spend a few hours or days in the most genial of company; walking in the Lake District is an addiction that is difficult to explain, but there for all to see.

Walkers in search of solitude these days will need to know their way around the Lake District extremely well. One Monday at the beginning of February, in misty conditions on the remote Caldbeck Fells, I encountered eight other people – two fell runners and three couples; on a bitterly cold day in January, as I parked up at 8am at Little Town in the Newlands Valley, three other cars were ahead of me, engines warm, occupants away on the fells.

But there are countless places where you can relax peacefully listening to nature in the raw, enjoying the view, watching the Lakeland world go by – in this book, I've identified just a few.

With the introduction of **'gps enabled' walks,** you will see that this book now includes a list of waypoints alongside the description of the walk. We have included these so that you can enjoy the full benefits of gps should you wish to. Gps is an amazingly useful and entertaining navigational aid, and you do not need to be computer literate to enjoy it.

GPS waypoint co-ordinates add value to your walk. You will now have the extra advantage of introducing 'direction' into your walking which will enhance your leisure walking and make it safer. Use of a gps brings greater confidence and security and you will find you cover ground a lot faster should you need to.

For essential information on map reading and basic navigation, read the *Pathfinder Guide Map Reading Skills* by outdoor writer, Terry Marsh (ISBN 978-0-7117-4978-8). For more information on using your gps, read the *Pathfinder Guide GPS for Walkers*, by gps teacher and navigation trainer, Clive Thomas (ISBN 978-0-7117-4445-5). Both titles are available in bookshops or can be ordered online at www.totalwalking.co.uk

1 *Newlands Valley*

START Little Town
DISTANCE 1½ miles
(2.4km)
TIME 1 hour
PARKING Parking area
adjacent to Chapel
Bridge, Little Town
ROUTE FEATURES Fell and
farm tracks; one stream
crossing; some boggy
ground

The Newlands Valley is rather less well known than most Lakeland dales, and is often used merely as a through route to Buttermere. But the valley has a fascinating legacy of industry, it is a sanctuary of the beautiful red squirrel and a perfect place to unwind and relax in relative solitude.

Leave the parking area beside Chapel Bridge and, climbing gently, walk along the lane towards Little Town. As soon as the fence on the right ends, however, leave the lane by crossing a step-stile on the right to gain a rising, stepped path to a higher and more substantial track that heads south (right) to the dale head.

Follow the track as it ambles along agreeably until, below Lowthwaite Crag, the intake wall of Low Snab Farm abruptly changes direction. **A** Turn right, with the wall,

crossing a short stretch of boggy ground to a footbridge spanning the infant beck, and climb on the other side to another broad track, this time below a large spread of scree on the fellside. Turn right, along the track.

The scree issues from the workings of an old mine, **Goldscope**, a name that first appears in records in 1569, during the reign of Elizabeth I. Goldscope is a corruption of 'Gottesgab' or 'God's gift', so called because it was one of the most prosperous mines in Lakeland.

PUBLIC TRANSPORT None
REFRESHMENTS Teas, Low Snab Farm; pubs in Braithwaite; full facilities for all the family in Keswick
PUBLIC TOILETS None on route or nearby
ORDNANCE SURVEY MAP Explorer Map OL4 (The English Lakes – North Western area)

Copper was mined here as early as the 13th century from a vein 9¾ft (3m) thick and exceptionally rich in workable copper. The mine also produced large quantities of lead, a small amount of silver and, allegedly, a modicum of gold.

The mine's greatest period of production was in the 16th century, when Queen Elizabeth I, concerned that the country should be less dependent on foreign supplies, made a serious attempt to exploit Britain's own resources. Ironically, it was imported German miners who largely worked Goldscope,

and production was encouraged by the award of hidden subsidies in the form of waived taxes.

Ore was taken by packhorse to the shores of Derwentwater, almost certainly across Chapel Bridge or its predecessor, and by way of Little Town. It was later transported to a smelter on the shores of the River Greta, at Brigham, and, having passed through Brigham, the copper then had to receive the

GPS WAYPOINTS

| 🖉 | NY 232 194 | Ⓑ | NY 230 193 |
| Ⓐ | NY 231 184 | | |

Queen's Mark, given at the Receiving House, now the Moot Hall in Keswick.

Continue forward along the track and through a gate into the farmyard at Low Snab. A permissive path now runs out from the farm to a junction near to Newlands Chapel .

The tiny chapel at Newlands was noted by **Wordsworth** in May 1826, who was struck by the appearance of the church gleaming through a veil of half-opened leaves. Much of the present building is Victorian, and the chapel retains a delightful simplicity, adjoined as it is by the old schoolroom, a place for quiet reflection.

At the junction near the church, turn right and follow the lane back to Chapel Bridge, beyond which lies the starting point of the walk at the car park. ●

? *What was the building adjoining Newlands Chapel used for?*

Newlands Valley from Cat Bells

Brothers Water

2

START Cow Bridge, Patterdale
DISTANCE 2½ miles (4km)
TIME 1½ hours
PARKING Cow Bridge car park
ROUTE FEATURES Woodland tracks, slippery when wet; lakeside path with tree roots to cross

Said to be named after two brothers who drowned there, Brothers Water is a small and usually tranquil lake, reflecting the surrounding fells. Its banks provide plenty of opportunity for a picnic in agreeable surroundings, enlivened especially in spring by the sound of birdsong – wood and willow warblers, chiffchaff, whitethroat, pied flycatchers, redstart and visiting cuckoos.

Leave the car park and cross the nearby bridge spanning Goldrill Beck, and turn left through a gate giving onto a broad, stony track. The track, never far from water, runs along the bottom edge of well-established woodland in which oak and beech predominate.

Gradually, the path rises gently, away from the water's edge, and, beyond the southern end of the lake, continues above broad alluvial pastures to reach Hartsop Hall Farm Ⓐ and Dovedale Cottage.

Follow the track past the farm and, ignoring paths going off to the

Hartsop Hall is a working farm, built originally in the 16th century, though it has been extensively rebuilt and altered since. It was formerly the home of the de Lancasters, and later of Sir John Lowther, who became the first Viscount Lonsdale at the end of the 17th century. When the hall was extended in the 18th century, it was built across an ancient right of way, a right which at least one dalesman insisted on exercising, by walking through the hall.

PUBLIC TRANSPORT All year and seasonal bus services daily to Patterdale from Windermere
REFRESHMENTS Brothers Water Inn, and in Patterdale
PUBLIC TOILETS None on route
ORDNANCE SURVEY MAP Explorer Map OL5 (The English Lakes – North Eastern area)

Syke Side Farm was the home of a character known as 'Old Charlie Dixon'. Charlie never left the Lake District, but was known worldwide as the Westmorland shepherd, a man who posed for many of the most famous pastoral photographs taken during the 'Box Brownie' era. He died in 1936 at the age of 83.

track, and go past the shop and farm buildings, bearing left at a Y-junction near the Brothers Water Hotel. Follow a driveway until, just as it reaches the road, leave it for a gate on the left giving on to a permissive path signposted for Brothers Water.

right, swing round to the left, in front of the hall, and then follow a track, right, over a cattle-grid and walk along a level track towards a caravan and camping site at Sykeside Farm **B**.

Continue through the site on a surfaced

GPS WAYPOINTS

📷 NY 403 134   **B** NY 403 119
A NY 398 120

Hartsop – cottage with spinning gallery

shoreline of Brothers Water. At various spots here the shoreline would be an ideal place for a picnic.

Gradually the path leaves the waterside and rises to a gate giving access to the road. Turn left and cross to a footpath opposite, and follow the road back to the Cow Bridge car park at the start of the walk.   ●

Initially the path hugs the road wall, and soon reaches a gap where, for a few strides, it adjoins the road. Then it descends to the

> **?** *How many different species of birds can you spot in the woodland along the first part of this walk?*

Brothers Water, looking towards Place Fell

3 *Tarn Hows by Tom Gill*

START Glen Mary Bridge, Tilberthwaite

DISTANCE 1½ miles (3km)

TIME 1 hour

PARKING Parking area at the foot of Tom Gill

ROUTE FEATURES Woodland paths; tarnside track

Enormously popular, and deservedly so, Tarn Hows may be approached from numerous directions, but this walk offers an ascent through delightful oak woodland turning to birch in the higher reaches. Attractive waterfalls enliven a route already rich in wildlife interest, especially in spring.

Start from the parking area at the foot of Tom Gill, and cross the nearby footbridge, turning right through a gate and ascending a steadily rising track alongside the stream.

The path, obvious all the way, passes a few low cascades as it goes up through predominantly oak woodland, but higher up it meets some more substantial falls **Ⓐ**, with the path being signposted along a ledge above the stream.

Above the falls a kissing-gate gives into the upper woodland, now mainly birch. The path ascends the whole time but at an easy angle, and eventually pops out onto a broad and level track at the edge of Tarn Hows.

Ⓑ Turn left and follow the main track all the way round Tarn Hows, ignoring branching paths on the left.

Although still known as **Tom Gill**, poet John Ruskin, who lived above the shores of Coniston Water at **Brantwood**, renamed Tom Gill as Glen Mary, which explains the name of the bridge at the foot of the stream.

PUBLIC TRANSPORT Daily bus services to Tom Gill, and seasonal National Trust 'Tarn Hows Tourer'

REFRESHMENTS Coniston

PUBLIC TOILETS Coniston; none on route

ORDNANCE SURVEY MAP Explorer Map OL7 (The English Lakes – South Eastern area)

🖍 SD 321 998	Ⓑ SD 327 998
Ⓐ SD 324 999	Ⓒ SD 333 999

Tarn Hows boasts a pristine beauty whatever the time of year, and is one of the loveliest spots in Lakeland, making it all the more difficult to accept that it was created artificially in the 19th century by damming a beck.

On the far side of the tarn, when the track forks Ⓒ, take the lower, right-hand branch, continuing parallel to the shoreline (sign-posted for Coniston and Yewdale). The track forks again just before

? Is Tarn Hows a real lake?

reaching a road. Branch right, and follow a gently descending path back to the top of Tom Gill. Turn left, and retrace the upward route, back to the foot of Tom Gill and the starting point. ●

Tarn Hows

4 *Barrow*

START Braithwaite
DISTANCE 3½ miles (5.6km)
TIME 2 hours
PARKING Parking area on Whinlatter road, above the village
ROUTE FEATURES Steadily rising fell path; rocky ridge and long grassy descent

The diminutive Barrow occupies an enviable position on the edge of the Newlands Valley, with a view from its summit ridge, overlooking the Vale of Keswick, that is as fine as any in Lakeland. A full frontal assault on the fell is the normal line of ascent, but this walk makes a less demanding approach before reaching the top of the fell and its 'surprise' view. A clear day is advised.

Leave the car park and turn right to go down the road into

The village of **Braithwaite** is where the renowned Cumberland Pencil Company was formed in 1868, before moving to its site in Keswick 30 years later when the buildings burned down. Braithwaite today is a quiet place with few residents employed locally, but in the past it had more than 1,000 inhabitants and its own coterie of tradespeople – butcher, baker, blacksmiths, millers, shoemaker, grocer, joiners and builders – and was closely associated with the village of Thornthwaite to the north.

Braithwaite. Take the first road on the right, crossing a stone bridge (High Bridge), and bear right, past Braithwaite Common – where there used to be a flour mill – and the Methodist church. Then leave the surfaced lane, on the left, for a brief stony track to the Coledale Inn, rejoining the surfaced lane beside the inn Ⓐ.

Near the start of this walk you pass Braithwaite Common. Why do you think it was called a 'common'?

PUBLIC TRANSPORT Daily bus services to Braithwaite
REFRESHMENTS Braithwaite has a couple of family friendly pubs; otherwise Keswick has a full range of facilities
PUBLIC TOILETS Braithwaite (on road between village and main road)
ORDNANCE SURVEY MAP Explorer Map OL4 (The English Lakes – North Western area)

continues beyond across open country, flanked by bracken.

The track rises steadily above the surprisingly deep ravine of Barrow Gill, and then moving away from the gill, becomes a broad grassy track, now with Grisedale Pike in view on the right. Outerside also comes into view ahead, to the right

Go forward along the lane, passing in front of the inn, and curving round to ascend gently towards High Coledale Farm. At a gate the surfacing ends, and a rough track

GPS WAYPOINTS

📝 NY 227 237	Ⓑ NY 224 225
Ⓐ NY 231 235	Ⓒ NY 234 229

Barrow WALK 4 **19**

Barrow from Coledale Beck

Continue across the top of Barrow and begin descending on a rocky path. Lower down the path becomes broad and grassy, through bracken, and is a delight to walk, though it can be slippery when wet. Halfway down the ridge there is a small dip, a miniature pass, close by which there are old mine workings.

of the pyramidal Stile End.

B At the foot of Stile End the path forks. Stay on the more pronounced track, branching left to pursue a gently rising path to the hause (Barrow Door) between Stile End and Barrow.

At Barrow Door, go left on a clear path climbing onto Barrow through heather and low rock outcrops. The stony path rises easily and soon reaches the top of Barrow, which has a grandstand and unrivalled view of the northern fells, the north-western fells, Newlands valley, Derwent Water and the long line of the Dodds and Helvellyn ranges. It comes as a surprise that such a modest fell can prove to be such an excellent vantage point, and this alone makes this walk especially worthwhile.

C When you reach the bottom of the path from Barrow (low sign-post nearby), go left on a grassy track descending to a gate at a wall end. Through the gate walk ahead to Braithwaite Lodge Farm, and then follow its access track which leads out into the village of Braithwaite.

As you meet the village lane, turn left, and then left again immediately before hump-backed Low Bridge in the village centre. Walk beside Coledale Beck, and soon bear right, near a post box, to rejoin the outward route at Braithwaite Common. Over High Bridge, turn left and go back up the road to the start. ●

Whinlatter Forest

START Whinlatter Visitor Centre
DISTANCE 1½ miles (2km)
TIME 45 minutes – 1 hour
PARKING Whinlatter Visitor Centre (Pay and Display)
ROUTE FEATURES Steep forest paths and tracks

5

The great spread of Thornthwaite Forest, part of the larger Whinlatter Forest, climbs to the lovely viewpoint of Lord's Seat, too distant a prospect for this walk, but typical of the many viewpoints that occur throughout the forest, offering cameo glimpses of soaring fells and lush valleys.

Leave the car park by walking up to the visitor centre, and there turn left onto a track (signposted 'Trails'), turning right a few strides later (also signposted 'Trails') onto a rising gravel path. Go up past a red, blue and green waymark.

At a path T-junction, turn right, still following the red, blue and green trail. Shortly, at another junction, keep left to reach a three-way junction, at a signboard on the left bearing the representation of a deer. Here, turn left, climbing energetically.

In Whinlatter Forest

PUBLIC TRANSPORT Daily bus service, April–October, to Whinlatter Visitor Centre from Keswick, Buttermere and Borrowdale
REFRESHMENTS Whinlatter Visitor Centre
PUBLIC TOILETS Whinlatter Visitor Centre
ORDNANCE SURVEY MAP Explorer Map OL4 (The English Lakes – North Western area)

GPS WAYPOINTS

NY 207 246

At the next junction, when the track forks, bear right, climbing steeply, to another sign with a heron on it. Here, as the track forks, bear left, leaving the main path, and climb to meet a forest trail at a welcome bench, from which there is a view across the valley to Grisedale Pike and Hobcarton End.

From the bench take the right-hand one of four possible tracks, and descend to a green waymark about 40 yds (36m) distant. At the waymark, leave the main track by turning right onto a constructed

> **?** *What are the main types of trees you will find in Whinlatter Forest?*

pathway into the forest, which soon starts to descend steeply.

The descending path leads down to another clearing/viewing area, with a sign nearby bearing a snail. The viewing takes in the Helvellyn range and Hospital Fell, a northerly continuation of Grisedale Pike.

Hospital Fell is named after an isolation hospital for sailors with tuberculosis.

> The view across to Helvellyn overlooks the **Vale of Keswick**, a lush, low-lying area with an extensive pattern of fields, hedgerows, trees and small woods that shelter the market town of Keswick. This valley pattern contrasts with the high open fells behind, among which Helvellyn is one of Lakeland's small number of summits to exceed 3,000ft (915m).

From the viewing area, keep left, descending on a red and blue trail. This leads down to meet a broad, forest trail. Turn left, climbing gently to a red and blue waymark about 100 yds (91m) away. At the waymark, leave the main trail, and descend, right, on the blue trail.

The blue trail goes down agreeably amid, in spring, much birdsong, to meet another main forest track, at which turn right, bringing you now onto the red trail, a broad forest track.

The descending track leads to a junction with a signpost numbered 14 nearby. Here, turn right to remain on the broad trail, which reunites the red and blue trails, and eventually leads back to the visitor centre and the starting point of the walk. ●

Whinlatter Forest in winter

6 *Loughrigg Tarn*

START Silverthwaite	
DISTANCE 2.8 miles (4.5km)	
TIME 1½ hours	
PARKING Silverthwaite parking area (Pay and Display)	
ROUTE FEATURES Narrow paths through bracken; rough tracks and lanes	

Beyond the brief initial pull up a brackeny slope, this walk soon becomes delightfully agreeable, wandering around popular Loughrigg Tarn before heading down to the valley to finish alongside the foaming River Brathay. There are viewing platforms for those who want a closer look at the splendid Skelwith Force, though young children should not be allowed to use them unattended, and preferably not at all.

From the car park a permissive path runs up alongside the garden wall of Silverthwaite Cottage. It climbs steeply for a short while, and affords a fine view of the Langdale Pikes.

At a cross-path, go forward and follow an obvious route around the north-western shoulder of Little Loughrigg to reach a cottage (Crag Head), and gain your first view of Loughrigg Tarn.

Ⓐ Descend to the left of the cottage, immediately bearing left onto a vehicle access track which leads to a surfaced lane.

Turn left for about 150 yds (138m), and there leave the lane, at a signposted footpath, by crossing a step-stile on the right into a sloping pasture. Head down-field on a grassy path to a ladder-stile. Over this, go forward, taking the higher of two green paths, to a gate giving onto a rough track.

Ⓑ Through the gate, turn right and follow the track to a gate beside a cottage. Through the gate,

PUBLIC TRANSPORT Daily bus service between Ambleside and Langdale
REFRESHMENTS Pub at Skelwith Bridge and café in Kirkstone Galleries
PUBLIC TOILETS None
ORDNANCE SURVEY MAP Explorer Map OL7 (The English Lakes – South Eastern area)

when the continuing track forks, branch right past Dillygarth Cottage, and soon reach a surfaced lane.

Turn left descending to a road junction. Turn right, soon crossing a stream near another road junction.

C Bear right, and continue following the road and, near the top of a rise, leave it, by turning left onto the rough track (signposted to Skelwith Bridge) to Crag Head used on the outward part of the walk.

At Crag Head, keep forward, following a path through bracken-clad hummocks dotted with low rock outcrops, to a gate giving into the larch woodland of Neaum Crag. A gravel path leads forward to the edge of a holiday park of wooden chalets.

Keep ahead, descending on a service road, the onward route waymarked by yellow arrows.

GPS WAYPOINTS

📄 NY 341 037	**C** NY 346 040
A NY 341 042	**D** NY 344 035
B NY 345 046	

The falls of **Skelwith Force** make a tremendous spectacle when in spate. Here the underlying rock drops 20–30ft (6–9m) in dramatic fashion, almost invariably providing a white-water show. Metal walkways lead down to a better viewing position, though *they are not suitable for unattended children.*

At a junction, go forward, and, immediately after a sleeping policeman, keep right of a chalet called 'Angle Tarn'.

Pass another – 'Yew Tree Tarn' – and head for a waymarked path enclosed by a low fence.

The path leads to a gate, go left on a path sandwiched between a wall and fence, which eventually gives

Loughrigg Tarn

into an open field. Keep forward, descending, and head for a kissing-gate giving onto the main road below.

D Through the gate, turn left and cross the road with care, turning right at the nearby road junction, and shortly, just before Skelwith Bridge, right again alongside the River Brathay, heading for the Kirkstone Galleries. At the entrance to the galleries, bear right and walk through the workshops

> **?** *The falls of Skelwith Force are spectacular, but what is the name of the river?*

to a riverside path beyond. Go along the path, passing the falls of Skelwith Force, and continuing to a gate which gives onto a large and flat pasture. Follow the main path beside the river, gradually circling round to draw level with a small knoll crowned by a stand of trees. Leave the main path here, by turning right onto a narrow path, passing to the right of the knoll and continuing to a gate giving into woodland. A gravel path now leads up through trees to the valley road, emerging directly opposite the Silverthwaite car park. Cross the road with great care. ●

Grizedale Forest

START Grizedale Visitor Centre

DISTANCE 3 miles (4.8km)

TIME 2 hours

PARKING Grizedale Visitor Centre car park (Pay and Display)

ROUTE FEATURES Woodland tracks and stony paths

A perfect place to wander in the off-season, when the forest is less well populated, but its beauty and wildlife remain. Numerous sculptures are dotted along the trail, some offering scope for the expression of musical talent, others leaving you to scratch your head! The woodland birdlife is also impressive.

Begin by walking past the Guardian of the Forest to the main road. Turn right for a short distance, taking care against approaching traffic and, at the first building on the left, cross the road and turn left onto a rising stony path. This is an unclassified road, and sometimes used by off-road vehicles: take great care should any approach.

Continue climbing, passing a few interesting sculptings – a quarry structure, larch wave seat and blind wall – on the way, with conditions underfoot improving gradually. The ascending track eventually

Guardian of the forest, Grizedale

PUBLIC TRANSPORT None, except the post bus

REFRESHMENTS Grizedale Tea Room

PUBLIC TOILETS Adjoining visitor centre

ORDNANCE SURVEY MAP Explorer Map OL7 (The English Lakes – South Eastern area)

merges with a broad forest trail. Keep right, and follow the trail to a T-junction.

At the junction, turn left, and continue with the trail, rising to a prominent Red Sandstone Fox Ⓐ. Here the trail forks. Branch right, climbing gently, and keep an eye open for a 'Feathersaurus' among the trees!

Continue following the green and white trails for some distance until they fork at an obvious Y-junction. At this point, turn left onto a narrow forest path that leads to hidden Grizedale Tarn Ⓑ. Then return to the main route.

The blue trail is known as the **Ridding Wood Trail,** and is surfaced throughout. It contains 20 pieces of contemporary forest sculpture, most of which are encountered in the final stages of this walk. This stretch will appeal especially to young children, for there is ample opportunity for musical expression here, concealed animals in the undergrowth to find, marimbas on which to play a tune, a buzzing hive and shadow faces in the forest – and there are quite a few places for mums and dads to relax, too.

GPS WAYPOINTS

📍 SD 335 944   Ⓑ SD 346 944
Ⓐ SD 345 952

Red Sandstone Fox, Grizedale Forest

Keep following the white trail now, which shortly leaves the main forest trail for a narrower, stony path. The path descends to a stream, crossed on wooden 'stepping stones'.

Eventually the path goes down steps to meet another broad forest trail. Turn left, and when the white trail leaves this main track, branch right onto it, now descending again on a narrow stony path.

When the white trail merges with the blue trail, take the lower of two paths (though it matters little

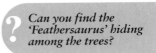

Can you find the 'Feathersaurus' hiding among the trees?

which path is taken, except that the lower route has the advantage in that it visits a number of woodland works of art).

Follow the blue trail to the new Education Centre and out across a car park to a road crossing point giving back into the grounds of the Visitor Centre to conclude the walk.

8 *Latterbarrow*

START Hawkshead

DISTANCE 3½ miles (5.6km)

TIME 2 hours

PARKING Hawkshead main car park (Pay and Display)

ROUTE FEATURES Good paths and tracks; muddy woodland trails; some stiles to cross

A splendid panorama is the reward for anyone who climbs Latterbarrow. This approach takes advantage of an old bridle-way across the northern slopes of Claife Heights, before swinging back to visit this popular summit.

Leave the village car park by its vehicular entrance, turn right to a T-junction and then left onto the Sawrey road. At the first junction, branch left along a narrow lane (signposted to Wray and Wray Castle). Follow the lane to Colthouse, taking care against approaching traffic, in the absence of roadside footpaths.

The tiny hamlet of **Colthouse** seems a peaceful place, as indeed it is, overshadowed by the glitzy (by comparison) glamour of nearby Hawkshead. But Colthouse was one of the remote communities visited by George Fox in 1653, following which the hamlet became an important Quaker centre – it still has a Friends' Meeting House. Another claim to fame is that William Wordsworth lodged here, while attending school in the village of Hawkshead.

Pass through this pleasant hamlet and continue northwards for about 250 yds (229m) beyond the last buildings to a signposted bridleway on the right, opposite the entrance to Gillbank **A**. Leave the road here, turning acutely right, through a gate onto a rising stony track. After a few yards, when the track forks, branch right.

PUBLIC TRANSPORT Daily and seasonal bus services to Hawkshead from Ambleside and Coniston

REFRESHMENTS Hawkshead has numerous family-friendly pubs and cafés

PUBLIC TOILETS Adjoining car park

ORDNANCE SURVEY MAP Explorer Map OL7 (The English Lakes – South Eastern area)

The ongoing track, climbing steadily throughout, continues for quite some distance as it crosses the wooded landscape between Latterbarrow and Colthouse Heights for a little over one mile (1.6km), for the most part in and out of mixed woodland. There are a few branching tracks, but the main line is obvious, following a course that is roughly east.

At a wall corner **B**, pass through a gate and onto a stony track at a forest boundary to a wall gap

Latterbarrow: the massive summit cairn

with a three-way signpost nearby. Here turn left on a clear path across a large area that has been storm damaged and cleared. On the far side, a stepped path leads up to another wall gap. Through the gap, turn right beside the wall and shortly swing left, once more across cleared ground, following a path that eventually leads back into forest. A path now leads along the forest boundary to a step-stile in a corner.

Over the stile turn sharply right to ascend Latterbarrow on a steadily rising track that leads directly to the enormous monument crowning the summit **C**.

From the summit take a direct line from the top of the fell – a grassy path – aiming for the distant village of Hawkshead to the south-west. Lower down the path joins another, and leads down to a country lane. Turn left for about 50 yds (46m) and then right into Loanthwaite Lane, where care is needed against approaching traffic.

After a little under 1/2 mile (800m), near farm buildings, take the second of two signposted footpaths

> As a viewpoint, the top of **Latterbarrow** is as good as any in Lakeland, especially so northwards across Ambleside at the head of Windermere and the ring of summits flanking Fairfield.

close together on the left (for Hawkshead), and use this to follow a surfaced route through meadows to reach Scar House Lane, in reality an enclosed, rough track.

Turn left, and very soon go right into another meadow, with Hawkshead plainly visible ahead. The continuing path leads un-erringly back towards Hawkshead. At the first of the cottages on the edge of the village, turn right over a bridge spanning a stream, and go along an enclosed path that curves around buildings and eventually emerges onto a main road.

> **?** Can you guess the height of the obelisk on the top of Latterbarrow?

Cross the road, continuing ahead on cobbles past attractive cottages and through an archway to arrive at the rear of the Kings Arms Hotel in the Square, which is entered via an archway.

William Wordsworth attended grammar school here from 1779 until 1787, when he went to St John's College, Cambridge. The

A view of Hawkshead

village, in spite of today's tourist trappings, has an air of peace and oneness with nature that would surely have impressed itself on the young boy's mind.

The village is also associated with Beatrix Potter, who lived only a few miles away at Hill Top Farm, near Sawrey, for it was here that her husband, solicitor William Heelis, had his office, which is now the Beatrix Potter Gallery.

Turn left and follow the road out of the village, to reach the turning into the car park in Hawkshead, back at the starting point of the walk. ●

Hawkshead is a timeless place of considerable character. The village developed at the junction of packhorse trails that were used to link the Windermere ferries with the Coniston valley.

9

Orrest Head and Allen Knott

START Windermere (near station)

DISTANCE 4½ miles (7.2km)

TIME 2 hours

PARKING Lay-by near Windermere Hotel, on A591

ROUTE FEATURES Woodland paths; farm tracks and fields

For all its modest height, Orrest Head provides one of the finest panoramas in Lakeland, rising only a short distance from the centre of Windermere. While walkers can easily return from the summit, this walk ventures farther, across farmland to Allen Knott, site of an Iron Age hillfort.

Directly opposite the National Westminster Bank on the main road through Windermere (A591), take the signposted path (a surfaced lane) for Orrest Head. The lane climbs initially quite steeply through light, mixed woodland, winding ever upwards. At the end of the surfaced lane, go forward onto a rough track. When the track forks at a bench, branch right.

Where the track swings round to run alongside a wall on the left, leave it and continue on a gently rising path beside the wall. The path leads to a kissing-gate, beyond which a stepped track rises onto the summit of Orrest Head.

A From the top of Orrest Head set off roughly northwards, aiming for a conspicuous group of white farm buildings close by a small tarn

Orrest Head is a justly famous and splendid viewpoint, providing a panorama that embraces the Coniston Fells, the Langdales and the length of Windermere. The top of this little fell, according to Lakeland writer Harriet Martineau, used to be the residence of Josiah Brown, 'who amused himself...with welcoming beggars, whom he supplied with meat and lodging'. He called them his 'jolly companions'.

PUBLIC TRANSPORT Rail and bus services to Windermere

REFRESHMENTS Windermere has numerous pubs and cafés

PUBLIC TOILETS Adjoining Windermere station

ORDNANCE SURVEY MAP Explorer Map OL7 (The English Lakes – South Eastern area)

GPS WAYPOINTS

✐	SD 413 988	Ⓓ	NY 414 013
Ⓐ	SD 414 994	Ⓔ	NY 411 001
Ⓑ	NY 417 004	Ⓕ	SD 414 997
Ⓒ	NY 414 010		

From the summit of Orrest Head, how many of the fells on the other side of Windermere can you name?

below. A grassy path drops to a through-stile in a wall corner beside a gate and continues descending, crossing a sloping field before running beside a wall and striking across a field punctuated by low rock outcrops, eventually to reach a back lane.

Go right and about 200 yds (128m) farther on leave the road over a through-stile onto a path (sign-posted to Far Orrest). Keep to the right-hand field edge to a kissing-gate, cross a small enclosure to another gate, beyond which lies a small copse. This in turn gives into a larger field. Head forward to a wall corner, where a stile accesses the next field.

Follow the right-hand field margin, heading for a distant ladder-stile, and passing a lovely pollarded ash tree **B** on the way.

Over the ladder-stile, cross the

ensuing field half-right aiming for distant farm buildings. After another ladder-stile, continue towards the farm buildings on a vehicle track that leads to a kissing-gate. Go through this and another nearby, then turn left along a field edge, passing the farm buildings and then turning through another gate giving onto a walled track.

Turn right along the track, and at its end keep forward beside a wall across the base of high ground, Allen Knott **C**, on the right.

The continuing path leads to a gate at a wall corner. Through this keep forward, climbing gently on a grassy track before descending to a surfaced lane.

D At the lane, turn left, and, taking care against approaching traffic, follow the road. When it forks, branch left and descend to a signposted access for Far Orrest Farm, on the left.

Turn onto the access lane, cross a cattle-grid and, when the lane forks, branch left and continue up to Far Orrest Farm.

Pollarding involves cutting a tree 8–12ft (2–4m) above ground, and allowing it to grow again to produce successive crops of wood. Ash was once valued for its strength and elasticity, making it ideal for tool handles and oars, but it is more usual to see ash coppiced (cut nearer the ground) than as a pollard.

Keep left in front of the buildings to a couple of wide gates. Cross a step-stile on the right (signposted 'Windermere via Crosses') and a farm compound, and then walk out through a gate and along a vehicle track across two fields.

In the second field, the track runs beside a wall, but when it swings left, leave it at a stile and gate in a wall corner. Climb beside a wall, soon reaching more level ground. After a ladder-stile/gate, continue on the track beyond eventually emerging at cottages and going forward to a lane.

E Turn left and pass Crosses Cottage, and follow the lane to the next farm (Causeway). Opposite the farm entrance, turn right, through a gate and onto a walled track. When the track enters an open field, keep forward beside a wall.

F As the ongoing track moves away from the wall, stay with it, climbing to a distant ladder-stile/gate. Over this, keep right alongside a wall, continuing on a terraced green path with lovely views.

The path soon descends to a through-stile beside a gate, and gives into woodland. Almost immediately bear right on a descending track. When the track forks, bear right between walls. At a path T-junction, turn left alongside a high wall. The descending path finally emerges on the Orrest Head road, a short distance from the main road (A591) and the starting point.

Lake Windermere from Orrest Head

10 *Buttermere*

START Buttermere village
DISTANCE 4½ miles (7km)
TIME 2–2½ hours
PARKING Car park at rear of Bridge Hotel (seasonal charges)
ROUTE FEATURES Good paths throughout; a little road walking

This simple tour of Buttermere is one of the most popular short walks in Lakeland, suitable for any season. The first part wanders along the base of Burtness Wood, often alive with birdsong, and provides stunning views up the valley. The return leg continues to hug the shoreline, before breaking away as it approaches the village.

The **Fish Hotel** is renowned for the story of Mary Robinson, the Maid of Buttermere, who lived and worked at the hotel. Her story was brought to fame at the turn of the 18th century. She was later wooed by, and eventually married, John Hadfield, who turned out to be an impostor and who was later hanged at Carlisle for forgery.

Leave the car park and turn right, around the Fish Hotel to follow a broad track through gates.

Ignore the signposted route to Scale Force, continue along the broad track towards the lake's edge, then follow the line of a hedgerow to a bridge at Buttermere Dubs.

A Cross the bridge and go through a gate in a wall at the foot of Burtness Wood. Turn left on a track through the woodland that roughly follows the shoreline of the lake, finally emerging from Burtness Wood near Horse Close, where a bridge spans Comb Beck.

Keep on along the path to reach a wall leading to a sheepfold and a gate. Go left through the gate, cross Warnscale Beck and press on to Gatescarth Farm.

PUBLIC TRANSPORT Daily bus services (April–October) from Keswick, Whinlatter and Borrowdale
REFRESHMENTS Two pubs at Buttermere (both welcome children) and a café
PUBLIC TOILETS Adjoining car park
ORDNANCE SURVEY MAP Explorer Map OL4 (The English Lakes – North Western area)

GPS WAYPOINTS

🖊 NY 173 169	**Ⓑ** NY 194 149
Ⓐ NY 172 163	**Ⓒ** NY 186 157

Ⓑ At the farm take the gate marked 'Lakeside Path', and follow signs to reach the valley road. A short stretch of road walking, left on the B5289, now follows, along which there are no pathways.

As the road bends left, leave it for a footpath on the left (signposted Buttermere via Lakeshore Path). The path brings you to a step-stile into a field, beyond which it never

The village of Buttermere

The head of Buttermere Valley

? *Where do you think the name 'Buttermere' comes from?*

strays far from the shoreline and leads to a stand of Scots pine, near Crag Wood.

C Beyond Hassnesshow Beck, the path enters the grounds of Hassness, where a rocky path, enclosed by trees, leads to a kissing-gate. Here a path has been cut into the crag, where it plunges into the

lake below, and the path disappears into a short and dripping tunnel.

After the tunnel a gate gives access to a gravel path through a wooded pasture, beyond which a right turn onto a fenced path leads to a traditional Lakeland bridge of slate slabs.

A short way on, through another gate, a path leads on to Wilkinsyke Farm, and finally an easy walk out to the road, just a little way above the starting point at the Bridge Hotel. ●

The **tunnel** was cut by employees of George Benson, a 19th-century Manchester mill owner who then owned the Hassness Estate, so that he could walk around the lake without straying too far from its shore.

Rydal Water

START White Moss Common

DISTANCE 3½ miles (5.6km)

TIME 2 hours

PARKING White Moss Common (Pay and Display)

ROUTE FEATURES Riverside paths; fell tracks and fields; rocky shoulder

This easy walk around Rydal Water is immensely popular at all times of year, and a simple route to follow. Such uphill walking as there is only serves to provide superb vantage points from which to appreciate the loveliness that is Rydal.

Begin from White Moss Common car park and cross the road with care to a descending stepped path opposite onto White Moss Common. At the bottom of the steps take a path bearing right beside the River Rothay.

Ignore a river footbridge, but keep on through a gate into another pasture and progressing through gates eventually enter light woodland.

Within the woodland the path immediately forks. Branch left, climbing a little and continue to a second footbridge, spanning the outflow of Grasmere.

Ⓐ Cross the bridge and go up steps immediately facing. Turn left onto a higher path climbing to run alongside an intake wall and then on to meet a bridleway (blue waymark).

At this point the bridleway descends left between a fence and wall. Lower down a few stepping-stones take the route across an in-flowing stream beyond which it continues beside a wall. The path eventually descends to pass along the shoreline of Rydal Water, and to cross a low, rocky shoulder at the water's edge, on which care is needed.

PUBLIC TRANSPORT Daily and seasonal bus services stop at White Moss Common

REFRESHMENTS Both Rydal and nearby Grasmere have family-friendly pubs

PUBLIC TOILETS On White Moss Common (to the left)

ORDNANCE SURVEY MAP Explorer Map OL7 (The English Lakes – South Eastern area)

GPS WAYPOINTS

| 🖊 NY 348 066 | **B** NY 359 060 |
| **A** NY 344 060 | **C** NY 351 068 |

B Towards the far end of Rydal Water, at a wall corner, the path forks. Branch left, staying along the edge of the lake, to a metal kissing-gate giving into Rydal Woods.

Follow the continuing path through the woods, leaving at another kissing-gate.

The path leads to a footbridge spanning the Rothay. On the other side, go up to meet the main road. Cross the road with care to the footpath opposite, turning right.

At the first road junction, turn left on an ascending road to Rydal Mount, passing the delightful Church of St Mary.

? *Behind the church at Rydal is Dora's Field. Who was Dora?*

The Church of St Mary was built during the reign of George IV, of simple construction, with a tower, nave and chancel. William Wordsworth helped to choose the site for the church, but seems not to have been too impressed with the finished product.

Rydal is a scattered grey-stone village, and its lake was a favourite spot of the Wordsworths, who would often have a picnic on the island.

Rydal Mount was home to Wordsworth and his family from 1813 until his

The track is the old road between Rydal and Grasmere, and saw service as a **corpse road** in the days before Rydal church was built. Along the way, a coffin stone, on which bearers would rest coffins while having a breather, now serves as a welcome seat.

death in 1850. Socially the house was a significant step up for the poet, putting him on calling terms with the local gentry.

Continue past Rydal Mount, behind which turn left onto a bridleway (signposted for Grasmere). A few strides on, go left through a gate onto a rough stony track that eventually breaks out into light woodland cover.

The continuing track is never in doubt, and undulates along below the steepness of Nab Scar.

C Just after a gate, near an overhead power-line, and before reaching a stream with a cottage above, descend left between walls on a broad stony path beside the stream.

The path reaches a gate, beyond which a broad stony track leads on to pass a waterfall.

Continue out to meet the main valley road. Turn right, cross a stream bridge and soon bear right to walk back into the White Moss Common car park at the starting point of the walk.   ●

Rydal Water

12 *Silver Bay*

START Patterdale
DISTANCE 3½ miles
(5.6km)
TIME 2 hours
PARKING Pay and Display
car park opposite
Patterdale Hotel
ROUTE FEATURES Bracken
and juniper fell slopes to
cross; rocky descent to
Silver Bay

This walk above the eastern shoreline of Ullswater is one of the most dramatically beautiful walks in the Lake District combining the attractions of the lake, with its steamers and sailing boats, craggy fell-sides and views into the deep, penetrating valleys to the west. The return leg is a menu of changing vistas, maintaining interest throughout.

Leave the car park and turn left to pass the White Lion. Take the next turning on the left, a narrow lane leading to the hamlet of Rooking.

On entering the hamlet, bear left, as if heading for Side Farm. Shortly go through a fell-gate, following a path signposted for Angle Tarn and Boredale Hause.

Begin along the path, but in just a few strides turn left and then go forward along a grassy path rising through bracken. This climbs

Patterdale

PUBLIC TRANSPORT All year and seasonal bus services daily to Patterdale from Windermere
REFRESHMENTS Patterdale pubs serve bar meals and welcome children
PUBLIC TOILETS En route, opposite White Lion Hotel
ORDNANCE SURVEY MAP Explorer Map OL5 (The English Lakes – North Eastern area)

gently through quarry spoil to a small grassy platform where the track forks Ⓐ. Here, take the higher path (on the right) which soon reaches a man-made cave, but which, *for safety's sake, should not be investigated too closely!*

The path continues its northerly course, always some distance above a lower path along which the walk is concluded. With some undulation, the continuing path presses on to a grassy saddle to the right of the conspicuous cone of Silver Crag, shrouded like the adjacent fellsides in juniper bushes.

GPS WAYPOINTS

🔖 NY 397 159 Ⓑ NY 397 180
Ⓐ NY 398 165

B Just over the saddle a short diversion is possible, climbing left on a sketchy path through juniper bushes onto Silver Crag, to savour an outstanding view across Ullswater to the fells of the Helvellyn and Fairfield ranges. Retrace your steps to return to the saddle.

 Silver Bay, its sheltered beach and the adjacent craggy headland are easily reached from what is now the main path. Here is a splendid place to relax and enjoy a picnic before setting off back to Patterdale.

prominent cross-path just above Silver Bay. Turn left.

To return simply follow the path around Silver Crag, following its up-and-down course, in and out of small copses and around rocky ribs until finally the buildings at Side Farm are reached.

Turn right between farm buildings and follow a broad access track out to the main Patterdale road, crossing Goldrill Beck on the way.

? *The lake here is called Ullswater, but what is the name of the valley?*

Continue the descent, passing a small reedy tarn before engaging a stony path that leads down to a

At the main road, turn left to return to the start. ●

Ullswater

Rannerdale

START Cinderdale Common, Rannerdale
DISTANCE 4½ miles (7.2km)
TIME 2½ hours
PARKING Cinderdale Common
ROUTE FEATURES Good paths; fell ridge walking; steep, stony descent

13

Rannerdale is Lakeland's secret valley, a place where invading Normans were massacred and bluebells now grow in profusion. The descent from the top of Rannerdale Knotts is steep, slippery when wet, and goes down loose rock for a short while; *anyone feeling intimidated by this should simply retrace their steps along the ridge and down the valley – a not unpleasant compromise.* The descent should not be attempted by young or unattended children.

 Begin from the roadside parking area on Cinderdale Common, beneath the steep slopes of Grasmoor. Walk up beside Cinderdale Beck for 50 yds (46m) and then cross it at a convenient spot. Follow the broad track on the other side, heading towards the shapely outline of Rannerdale Knotts.

The track soon assumes a level course and reaches a gate beyond which it continues into the valley of Rannerdale, which has now opened up ahead.

As the path reaches the entrance to Rannerdale, go down to cross a footbridge spanning Squat Beck. **A** Turn left to a gate and take to the narrow path rising up into Rannerdale.

? *What wild flower, in particular, is Rannerdale famous for?*

PUBLIC TRANSPORT Daily bus services (April – October only) from Keswick
REFRESHMENTS Buttermere has two pubs and a café
PUBLIC TOILETS None on route
ORDNANCE SURVEY MAP Explorer map OL4 (The English Lakes – North Western area)

Rannerdale, for all its undoubted beauty, has something of a sinister history to it, for it was here, at the end of the 11th century, that the people of Buttermere ambushed and slew invading Normans, leaving their bodies to rot at the entrance to the dale.

The story is evocatively told in *The Secret Valley* by Nicolas Size, which relates how 'It was hopeless to try and bury great piles of Norman dead', and how Rannerdale 'was like a charnel house'. Today the spot where the Normans were left is said to burst each spring into an intensely bright carpet of bluebells, lending some truth, perhaps, to Omar Khayyam's notion the 'the loveliest flowers may spring from some dead Caesar's breast'.

Continue to follow the path all the way to the very highest point of the dale, a narrow col of land below the southern summit of Whiteless Pike and looking across the intervening valley to the steep slopes of Robinson.

B At the top of the dale, turn abruptly right

GPS WAYPOINTS

NY 162 192 **B** NY 179 177
A NY 168 186

and take to an undulating path that runs the length of the delightful ridge leading to the cairned top of Rannerdale Knotts.

Cinderdale Common

The ridge is broad and ranks among the finest ridge walks in Lakeland, so much so that to turn tail and walk back along it is very much a tempting proposition. *If there are young children in the party, it is essential that this option be adopted in preference to attempting the steep descent to the shores of Crummock Water, which can be very intimidating for a while.*

The way down keeps initially to the right of the top of Rannerdale Knotts and soon reaches a low col between the main summit and a minor top a little lower down. Here, turn left to continue the descent, which becomes increasingly steep and leads into a loose, rocky gully where hands, feet and bottoms will be brought into play.

At the bottom of the gully, continue forward a short distance, then swing left and right through bracken with the descending path, which heads down to cross the craggy slopes above Hause Point.

Continue descending, much more easily now, to reach the road. Turn right for a short distance, and turn into a parking area. Go through the parking area *(which can be used as an alternative start by anyone wanting to shorten this walk),* and follow a wall until it becomes possible to move away from it and to turn into the entrance to Rannerdale once more. This time there is a fine view of the many low cascades that enliven Squat Beck at this point.

Recross the footbridge over Squat Beck Ⓐ and retrace the outward route to Cinderdale Common. ●

14 *Castlerigg and Tewet Tarn*

Castlerigg Stone Circle is a popular place with visitors to the northern Lake District, and rightly so, its ancient stones are a great fascination. This walk starts and finishes close by them, but forms a wide loop to visit reedy Tewet Tarn and the isolated church of St John's in the Vale before trekking back across low-lying farmland.

START Castlerigg Stone Circle
DISTANCE 4 miles (6.4km)
TIME 2 hours
PARKING Roadside parking area adjoining Castlerigg
ROUTE FEATURES Back lanes; farm fields; access tracks; stiles and hummocky fellsides

Leave Castlerigg Stone Circle by walking east (away from Keswick) along the lane, but take care against approaching traffic. The road descends round a bend and soon reaches Goosewell Farm.

Go through a gate on the right (signposted) and cross to another a short distance away, then head down-field diagonally left, aiming for a distant bridge.

Pass through another gate and cross to a ladder-stile at a gate gap, then cross to a gate giving onto the lane crossing the bridge.

Ⓐ Turn right and cross the bridge. Follow the road to a T-junction and turn right, walking as far as the next junction on the right (signposted Shundraw and St John's in the Vale Church).

Ⓑ Turn right again, following this quiet lane, but once more taking care against approaching traffic.

After about 350 yds (320m), leave the lane at a five-bar gate on the right (signed to St John's in the Vale Church via Tewet Tarn). Through the gate, bear right, climbing gently on a grassy vehicle track to reach a wall gap at the top of the field.

PUBLIC TRANSPORT None
REFRESHMENTS Keswick has numerous family-friendly pubs and cafés
PUBLIC TOILETS None on route
ORDNANCE SURVEY MAP Explorer Map OL4 (The English Lakes– North Western area)

GPS WAYPOINTS

🔖 NY 293 237	ⓒ NY 304 233
Ⓐ NY 300 239	ⓓ NY 306 225
Ⓑ NY 304 240	ⓔ NY 290 225

Through the gap continue climbing beside a wall, and later bearing away from the wall to a signpost, beyond which Tewet Tarn comes into view.

Tewet (Tewit) Tarn is a small reedy pool set in a hollow, its waters often reflecting Lonscale Fell and Skiddaw to the north. This is a delightfully peaceful setting, far away from the hubbub of towns and busy valley roads.

From the signpost, cross a shallow ravine, and follow an indistinct grassy path across a pasture to a through-stile to the left of a wall gap. Over this, go forward on a broad grassy track to the right of the stile, which passes close by Tewet Tarn.

Beyond the tarn the path improves and leads to a step-stile over a fence Ⓒ. Ahead now is the rugged lump of Low Rigg, the next objective. A grassy path leads towards it, and passes just to the right of the summit.

Now the path scampers downhill to cross a wall at a through-stile, beyond which it continues through bracken, heading for a small cluster of buildings in the distance. As the buildings are approached, the path picks a way across wet ground to a through stile giving onto a surfaced lane at St John's in the Vale Church. The lane was once an important thoroughfare linking the valleys east and west with their church.

D Turn right, pass a Diocesan Youth Centre, and follow the lane to a distant gate. Beyond the gate a broad vehicle track descends, winding down, with widening views, to meet a surfaced lane near Sykes Farm.

At this junction, cross the lane to a kissing-gate nearby, and walk down field, following a green path. Soon the path reaches another kissing-gate at the bottom of the pasture.

In the ensuing field, head towards a gate on the right at the end of a wall (waymark). Do not go through the gate, but keep alongside the ongoing fence to another gate and fence at a wall corner.

Beyond this cross to a nearby footbridge and cross the next field on a grassy path to a distant signpost at which a vehicle track is met.

Turn right, signposted for Keswick, and walk to a five-bar gate in a wall corner. Through this continue up the right-hand field margin to a through-stile at the top. Follow a grassy track across the next field to a kissing-gate giving onto the busy A591.

E Turn right, and after 50 yds (46m), turn right again onto an access track to Low Nest Farm.

Immediately after crossing a cattle-grid, turn left through a kissing-gate, and walk up the ensuing field on a grassy path that leads to the access to High Nest Farm. Turn right and walk on to pass the farm

Castlerigg Stone Circle

buildings to a gate, and then keep forward on a muddy path parallel with the right-hand field margin. Keep to the field margin to reach a

Castlerigg Stone Circle is believed to pre-date the great circles at Stonehenge and elsewhere. It is commonly regarded as one of the most superb stone circles of the many to be found in Britain. Enthusiasts believe Castlerigg to be among the earliest stone circles in Europe, though poet John Keats was not impressed, describing the stones (in *Hyperion*) as 'a dismal cirque, Of Druid stones upon a forlorn moor'.

kissing-gate, then cross to another not far away, and repeat this in the next field.

Follow a green path across pasture, heading for a distant plantation. The path then runs past the woodland to meet a lane. Turn left here to return to the starting point of the walk. ●

? *According to the information boards, how old is Castlerigg Stone Circle?*

15 *Cat Bells*

Arguably the best known of the lower Lakeland fells: many a first, faltering step to fell-walking freedom was planted on the grassy slopes of Cat Bells, a summit that remains ever popular throughout the year for its outstanding views of Derwent Water, Borrowdale and the Newlands Valley.

START Hawse End

DISTANCE 3½ miles (5.6km)

HEIGHT GAIN 1,150ft (350m)

TIME 2 hours

PARKING Small wooded parking area at Hawse End

ROUTE FEATURES Steep ascent and descent; rocky outcrops

Begin from Hawse End (Hawes End on the map), where the road from Swinside and Portinscale makes a sharp zigzag before turning round the side of Cat Bells. Above the hairpin bend, at the junction for Skelgill, take a stepped path rising up the fellside.

Follow this through all its twists and turns, climbing steadily through grass and bracken to encounter a few small rocky outcrops before reaching the lower, northernmost summit of Cat Bells, sometimes called Brandlehow **A**.

The onward route is never in doubt, a broad trail keeping to the centre of a grassy ridge, before rising dramatically through more

The great expanse of **Derwent Water** lies directly below, while to the north the slaty slopes of Skiddaw soar above the market town of Keswick. Further right, the southern ridges of Blencathra overlook Glenderamackin Vale. To the east the Dodds lead into the Helvellyn range, while to the west graceful fells tumble along the skyline from Lord's Seat, across Grisedale Pike and Eel Crags to the high ground above unseen Buttermere beyond Robinson, Hindscarth and Dale Head.

PUBLIC TRANSPORT Derwent ferry to Hawse End all year; bus services to Hawse End (April – October) from Keswick, Borrowdale and Buttermere

REFRESHMENTS Portinscale and Keswick

PUBLIC TOILETS None on route

ORDNANCE SURVEY MAP Explorer Map OL4 (The English Lakes – North Western area)

rock outcrops to the cone of Cat Bells. *In a few places the path moves close to the grassy slopes, which will be slippery when wet, so care is needed until the summit is reached.* The final ascent is not so demanding as it appears when viewed end on.

The initial descent from Cat Bells involves

? *When you stand on the summit of Cat Bells, what is the name of the next mountain to the south?*

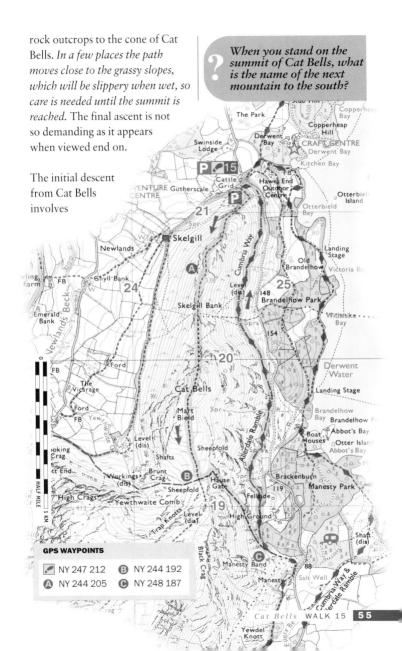

GPS WAYPOINTS

🖊 NY 247 212   **B** NY 244 192
A NY 244 205   **C** NY 248 187

Cat Bells WALK 15   **55**

negotiating its rocky summit ring before descending easily to the broad col of Hause Gate **B**. Here turn left, descending a constructed pathway towards the wooded area around Manesty below.

> **Brackenburn** was the sometime home of Sir Hugh Walpole (1884–1941), the English novelist, born in Auckland, New Zealand, who bought the property in 1923. His collection of works known as *The Herries Chronicle* is set in and around Borrowdale.

Keep descending to meet a broad track going left along the edge of woodland. (There are two earlier and higher shortcuts that meet this same track, though the higher of the two requires care in wet conditions.)

C Turn left, and follow the path above woodlands and the attractively set house of Brackenburn.

Press on beyond Brackenburn, the path soon dipping to make a brief acquaintance with the road at a small quarry car park. Beyond this gap, immediately return to a gently rising path, an old road, traversing the lower slopes of Cat Bells, that will ultimately bring you back to the road at Hawse End.

Cross the road and go down a brief shortcut to a gate near a cattle-grid, from which the parking area is soon reached. ●

En route to Cat Bells

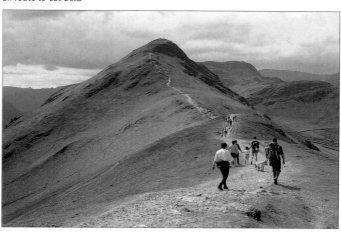

Blawith Common and Beacon Tarn

START Brown Howe, Coniston shore

DISTANCE 3½ miles (5.6km)

TIME 2½ hours

PARKING Brown Howe car park on shore of Coniston Water

ROUTE FEATURES Some busy road walking to start; brackeny fells, muddy when wet, and minor unenclosed road to finish

Concealed high among the brackeny folds of Blawith Common, the idyllic Beacon Tarn is a perfect spot for a picnic set against the magnificent backdrop of the Coniston and Dunnerdale Fells; a real eye-opener and an ideal place to find a little solitude.

Beacon Tarn

Leave the car park and turn left along the road. Cross the road and go past a road junction and,

for safety (but not of necessity), shortly afterwards take to a rough track ascending, on the right, towards a disused quarry.

Just before the quarry entrance, bear left onto a grassy path through bracken. This path, roughly parallel with the road below, involves dodging below branches, and shortly leads back down to the road.

Continue along the road, with great care, until, having passed two parking areas on the left (Blawith

PUBLIC TRANSPORT Daily bus services (Monday–Saturday, and summer Sundays) run along the A5084 from Coniston

REFRESHMENTS Pub in Torver, but otherwise Coniston has a host of family-friendly facilities

PUBLIC TOILETS Brown Howe car park

ORDNANCE SURVEY MAP Explorer Map OL6 (The English Lakes – South Western area)

GPS WAYPOINTS

| 📝 SD 291 911 | **B** SD 281 899 |
| **A** SD 286 902 | **C** SD 275 905 |

Common), a track is reached on the right, just as the road bends left. **A** The track rises steadily onto brackeny slopes.

Near overhead powerlines, the track forks **B**. Branch left, still climbing. Eventually the path crosses the shoulder of Slatestone Fell and descends to a path junction, close by a wooden footbridge.

Beacon Tarn is surprisingly large, almost a lake, and is the 'Trout Tarn' of Arthur Ransome's 'Swallowdale' (*Swallows and Amazons*, 1930), in which Roger was taught how to 'guddle' trout. North-east of the tarn rises Beacon Fell, a neat craggy summit with fascinating outcrops.

Turn right. The path continues through a landscape of undulating bracken hummocks punctuated by low, rock outcrops. When the path next forks, just by some stepping-stones bridging a stream, turn right, crossing the stones

? *When you reach Beacon Tarn, what is the name of the group of fells you can see in the distance across the tarn?*

and walking on to the edge of Beacon Tarn, which remains concealed until the very last moment.

Speculation invariably arises among readers of Ransome's tales about where, exactly, Swallowdale is. Of course, the author never disclosed his locations, but at Beacon Tarn you may be forgiven for thinking you are very close – something of a mystery, that can be resolved by reading the book itself.

At the water's edge, turn left. Across the next section numerous paths diverge, but the immediate objective is simply to walk around the tarn, keeping to an obvious path that leads the way – this is, in fact, part of the Cumbria Way, a popular Lakeland medium-distance walk.

Beyond the northerly edge of the tarn, a grassy path ascends through a gap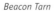

between low-lying fells, and provides outstanding views of the Coniston Fells ahead.

After the gap, the path descends steadily to pass a low-lying marshy area, and slips easily through another shallow col before moving out onto a broad expanse of mossland.

Gradually the path starts heading for the distant green cone of Coats Hill and the minor road by which the walk concludes. When the descending path forks, branch left, staying on the more prominent of the two paths.

Eventually, when the path meets the road, turn right, and follow it through an agreeable birch and ash landscape to meet the main road at a T-junction, only a short distance from the entrance to the Brown Howe car park. ●

Beacon Tarn

17 *Elterwater*

This delightful and easy walk meanders through farm fields and beside tarns, streams and rivers, with exquisite views of the surrounding fells. The going is nowhere difficult, and interest remains high throughout the walk.

START Elterwater village
DISTANCE 5½ miles (8.9km)
TIME 3 hours
PARKING Elterwater car park, just south of the Britannia Inn, or Elterwater Common, north of the village
ROUTE FEATURES Good paths all the way; spectacular waterfalls and riverside paths

🖉 Take the path to Skelwith (pronounced Skellith) Bridge from the river corner of the car park, a route initially requiring little description as it wanders on pleasantly to a superb resting place beside Elter Water **A**. The Langdale Pikes rise across the tarn, their crags and gullies often so vividly etched you feel you could reach out and touch them.

? *What kind of tree is it growing in front on the Britannia Inn in Elterwater village?*

Beyond the tarn, keep to the obvious path, passing through a gate close to the main road, and then pressing on soon to reach an attractive footbridge **B** spanning the River Brathay. Cross the bridge into

PUBLIC TRANSPORT Daily bus services run from Ambleside into Langdale
REFRESHMENTS Pubs at Elterwater and Skelwith Bridge, café at Kirkstone Galleries
PUBLIC TOILETS None
ORDNANCE SURVEY MAP Explorer Map OL7 (The English Lakes – South Eastern area)

GPS WAYPOINTS

✎ NY 328 048		**C**	NY 339 032
A NY 338 041		**D**	NY 328 031
B NY 341 035		**E**	NY 312 030

broad-leaved woodland, following a clear path that eventually leads round to join another, ascending from the left. Here, turn right, climbing gently through Bridge How Coppice.

At the top edge of the woodland, go through another kissing-gate and continue on an obvious stony path that soon meets a rough vehicle access track. Turn right,

following the track past a group of cottages and through two metal kissing-gates. The continuing path is obvious and leads to Elterwater

> The **river** flowing from Elter Water is the **Brathay**, which produces Skelwith Force, a tumult of foaming water in rich, green woods, and approached on metal walkways.

Park Country Guest House.

Set in the **stonework** of one of the buildings here is some of the handiwork of an apprentice stonemason – a homework exercise, perhaps?

C Leave the buildings behind by following a waymarked path descending to a step-stile, and on to a gap-stile in a field corner. This gives onto an enclosed path, at the end of which cross to a metal kissing-gate. Follow an obvious path across a sloping field to a step-stile perched dramatically above the River Brathay.

The path that follows skims along the top of a steep drop to the river before descending an awkward path to the riverside and crossing a small enclosure to a lane. Turn right for about 80 yds (74m), and then leave the lane, on the left, at a footpath signposted to High Park.

Cross two stiles adjoining the road and then bear immediately right on a permissive path to Colwith Force. As you approach, keep to the right of a fenced enclosure to reach a grandstand view of the falls **D**.

Retrace your steps and walk around the enclosure, climbing to cross a low shoulder high above the falls.

Now, follow a woodland path, initially parallel with the river, but then moving away from it to rise to a gate in a wall. Through this, follow the continuing wall and soon turn right to walk across to High Park Farm. There turn left and go up to a lane, turning right and following the lane to Stang

Slater Bridge, Little Langdale

End, where the road zigzags between buildings.

Stay on this quiet lane to the edge of woodland and then follow a broad track round to a footbridge spanning the Brathay. Do not cross the bridge, but instead go left beside the river on a rough track until, at a kissing-gate on the right, you can leave the track to approach nearby Slater Bridge **E**.

Colwith Force, one of Lakeland's secret waterfalls

Cross the bridge and keep straight ahead beside a wall on your right (ignoring gaps and diverting pathways). The path rises with the wall, and provides an outstanding view to your left of Little Langdale Tarn and Greenburndale beyond. The path leads up to a farm access. Turn left and walk out to the Little Langdale road.

Go left again and then immediately right onto a lane that after another farm degenerates into a rough, stony track.

Beyond a gate, as the track enters light woodland, keep right and continue descending, with increasing roughness underfoot, eventually to meet a lane leading out to the Elterwater road. Turn left to return to the village. ●

> **Slater Bridge** is a superb legacy of quarrying times, a cobbled, narrow construction leading to a slab bridge across the infant river.

18 *Grisedale*

START Patterdale
DISTANCE 6 miles (9.7km)
TIME 3 hours
PARKING Pay and Display car park opposite Patterdale Hotel
ROUTE FEATURES Fell paths, farm tracks and rugged mountain terrain

Many visitors to Lakeland use Grisedale as a through-route or for access to the high fells of the Fairfield and Helvellyn ranges. Here it is visited for its own intrinsic qualities of pastoral pleasantness and a taste of the mountains.

Turn left out of the car park and opposite the White Lion turn right onto a signposted path climbing past public toilets. At the rear of an isolated building, leave the track by turning left onto a signposted path through bracken and heather. This leads to a gate giving onto open fellside.

A path climbs rockily for a short while before descending to a kissing-gate to the left of two other gates.

PUBLIC TRANSPORT All year and seasonal bus services daily to Patterdale from Windermere
REFRESHMENTS Patterdale pubs (family-friendly); shop
PUBLIC TOILETS Opposite White Lion Hotel
ORDNANCE SURVEY MAP Explorer Map OL5 (The English Lakes – North Eastern area)

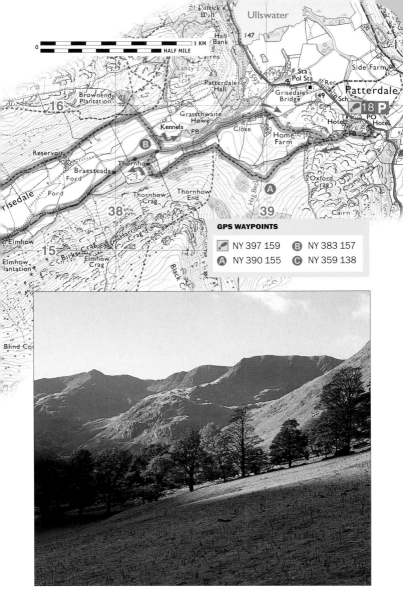

GPS WAYPOINTS

🖉 NY 397 159		B	NY 383 157
A	NY 390 155	C	NY 359 138

The view towards the head of Grisedale

Through this, follow the continuing wall, then climb to a horizontal path before descending gently to cross Hag Beck on stepping-stones **A**. The path continues easily, crossing the slopes of Glenamara Park and the steeper slopes below Thornhow End.

Follow the path as it runs alongside a wall bounding a pine plantation, and then maintain a level course as the wall drops away to the right. A short way on, the path rejoins a wall and then leads to a gate. Pass through this gate and continue descending beside a wall to a couple of sheepfolds. There turn right through a gate, going down-field, past a barn to a surfaced track.

B Turn left and follow the track up-valley. When it swings round to access Braesteads Farm, keep ahead onto a graded track to Elmhow Farm. After Elmhow Farm, the path becomes increasingly rugged as the route penetrates to

> **Intake walls** were built as the outer limits of valley farms, and are found everywhere throughout Lakeland. But the wall at the head of Grisedale is quite stupendous, and rises crazily onto the slopes of Striding Edge. Here especially it is a lasting testimony to a skilled and dying breed of men.

the heart of the high fells and into a harsher, mountain landscape.

> **?** *Many of the farm buildings along this walk have a pattern of holes high in their gable ends. What do you think they were for?*

Below Nethermostcove Beck, a footbridge may be used as a shortcut to the opposite bank, but otherwise continue climbing. There is increasing ruggedness underfoot until Grisedale Beck is crossed.

C A rough path leads on to join a path descending from nearby Ruthwaite Lodge. At this turning point, cross another footbridge and begin the return journey.

A good path now sweeps back down the valley, giving lovely views of waterfalls not seen on the ascent, and passing through the intake wall below Nethermostcove Beck.

Continue following the descending path, which re-ascends briefly after passing above Braesteads Farm. Eventually it reaches a wall corner, where there are two gates. Go through the right-hand one, and down-field to a surfaced farm access below.

Keep forward to cross Grisedale Beck, now a much quieter version of its ebullient former self. At a T-junction, turn left and follow a surfaced lane until it makes a pronounced left turn. Here leave it by branching right onto a wide track (signposted). Shortly, leave the track at a waymark, pass through a kissing-gate, and follow a waymarked route across rough pasture to a high through-stile in a wall. Over the wall, rejoin the outward route. Turn left to follow it back to the start.

The valley of **Grisedale** was fashioned along the line of a geological fault, but was once occupied by a huge glacier feeding into the main Patterdale glacier. By looking along the valley sides, a good idea can be gleaned of the depth of the glacier at this point. When the glacier retreated about 11,000 years ago, it started to deposit the heavy mountain debris it could no longer carry, and this collected into enormous piles of rubble known as moraine. Below Ruthwaite Lodge there are many examples of these hummocky moraines, remnants of that last Ice Age.

Central Grisedale

19 *Latrigg*

START Keswick (disused) railway station
DISTANCE 5 miles (8km)
TIME 3 hours
PARKING At railway station
ROUTE FEATURES Old railway trackbed; one steepish climb on country lane; grassy ridge and gradual descent

In spite of lying below the massive bulk of Skiddaw, Latrigg maintains a dominant position overlooking the market town of Keswick. The usual ascent involves continuous uphill walking, but here an approach is started along the trackbed of the former Penrith-Keswick-Cockermouth railway before slipping fairly easily onto the eastern end of Latrigg.

From the old Keswick railway station, head along the trackbed, which quickly leads away from Keswick to begin a gentle flirtation with the River Greta that continues throughout the early part of the walk.

The way forward is never in doubt, and just before the path passes beneath the elevated A66 an interesting milepost is encountered, one of 1,000 funded by the Royal Bank of Scotland to mark the creation of the National Cycle Network.

Where did this branch line start and finish? You'll find the answer on information panels along the walk.

PUBLIC TRANSPORT Numerous daily bus services to Keswick
REFRESHMENTS Keswick town centre has numerous family-friendly pubs and cafés
PUBLIC TOILETS At start
ORDNANCE SURVEY MAP Explorer Map OL4 (The English Lakes – North Western area)

GPS WAYPOINTS

📍 NY 272 237   🅱 NY 296 251
🅐 NY 286 241   🅒 NY 281 253

Having
passed under the
A66, the path then takes to an
attractive boardwalk section above
the river, before continuing to the
site of a former bobbin mill at Low
Briery 🅐.

The first bobbin mills in the Lake
District were opened during the
Industrial Revolution in response
to the growing demand from
cotton and woollen mills of the
North. At peak production, Low

Briery could produce over 40
million bobbins a year. The
bobbins at Low Briery were made
from coppiced ash, birch, lime,
sycamore and alder.

Low Briery is the site of an old
bobbin mill. Here the waters of
the River Greta have been used for
industrial purposes for over 600
years. In the early 19th century
there was a water-powered pencil
mill, several bobbin mills and a
specialist textile mill, known locally
as 'Fancy Bottoms Mill', which made
the intricate bottom edgings of
waistcoats.

Press on steadily to reach an old railway building on the right (just before a bridge), now used as an information point. Before reaching this, go through a gate on the left, and cross a narrow enclosure to a back lane.

Turn left and climb, a little steeply for a while. When the lane/track forks, branch left to a footpath sign (Skiddaw) at a gate and step-stile **B**. Go over a stile beside the gate onto a broad track swinging round gorse bushes, then running centrally up the eastern ridge of Latrigg.

A short way on a plantation is reached, on the right. Just before the end of the plantation, climb left to the centre of the ridge.

A fine promenade now leads across the top of Latrigg to the highest point (which is unmarked, save for a tiny rock outcrop), with stunning views of the Dodds, the central

Ascending onto Latrigg

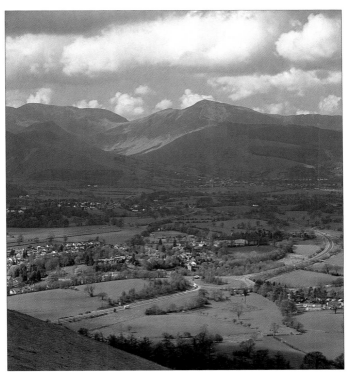

The Vale of Keswick from the summit of Latrigg

fells, those of the Newlands Valley and the North West, and, to the right, the massive bulk of Skiddaw, Little Man and Lonscale Fell.

From the high point turn northwards and follow a broad grassy track that gradually descends to the parking area at the top of Gale Road **C**. Go through a gate and into the parking area, but soon leave it for a path on the left (The Cumbria Way), that now follows a long, clear and steadily descending course all the way down to a gate at the end of Spooney Green Lane, which soon crosses high above the A66 and runs out to meet a back lane. Turn left and follow the lane, bearing right at a pronounced left bend to return to the railway station parking.

20 *Castle Crag*

START Seatoller, Borrowdale
DISTANCE 5 miles (8km)
TIME 2 –3 hours
PARKING National Trust car park at Seatoller (Pay and Display)
ROUTE FEATURES Stony tracks; rocky scrambling (optional); riverside paths; numerous tree roots and rocky sections; one brief, low rocky ledge to cross

Commanding a stunning view across Derwent Water to the smooth profile of Skiddaw, Castle Crag is too inviting a prospect to pass by (almost), but its conquest is held in reserve for those who can tackle its steep, slaty path (in both directions). Beyond, woodland wandering awaits, and a riverside amble as good as any in Lakeland.

Leave the car park and turn right to walk up through Seatoller village. Go past the National Park Information Centre at Dalehead Barn, which is well worth a visit, and go out of the village on the Honister road.

At the edge of the village, turn right at a gate giving onto a well-graded track that climbs easily onto the fellside above, heading for a group of four Scots pine, and then swings left to a gate.

Beyond the gate, continue climbing on a stony track, initially beside a wall, until it meets a steeper path ascending from Seatoller below. Go forward onto the middle one of three possible paths (yellow waymark), and ascend close-cropped turf to a gate in a wall corner.

Ⓐ Through the gate turn right onto a path alongside a wall, which gradually leads onward, crossing streams (by footbridges) in the process, to the foot of Tongue Gill, a prominent and deeply cleft valley on the left – once renowned for its quarries. Having gained consider-able height, the path affords an

PUBLIC TRANSPORT Bus services daily from Keswick to Seatoller
REFRESHMENTS Seatoller (café)
PUBLIC TOILETS Seatoller car park
ORDNANCE SURVEY MAP Explorer Map OL4 (The English Lakes – North Western area)

GPS WAYPOINTS

🖋 NY 246 138		🄲 NY 250 165	
🄰 NY 242 142		🄳 NY 252 151	
🄱 NY 247 157			

0 ———————— 1 KM
HALF MILE

airy, invigorating view of Borrowdale and its enclosing fells.

Beyond Tongue Gill, the path, which remains obvious throughout, heads for Castle Crag directly ahead and framed between distant views of Skiddaw (to the left) and Blencathra (to the right).

B The path starts to descend as it draws level with Castle Crag, and soon a path can be seen rising on the right just before an enormous spill of scree.

Leave the descending track at this point to cross to the path rising steeply, very steeply in places, onto Castle Crag.

? *Who gave Castle Crag to the National Trust?*

Visitors have been ascending **Castle Crag** for centuries, but none has described the view better than Thomas West in his *Guide to the Lake* published in 1778: 'From the top of Castlecrag in Borrowdale, there is a most astonishing view of the lake and vale of Keswick, spread out to the north in the most picturesque manner … a beautiful mixture of villages, houses, cots and farms, standing round the skirts of Skiddaw. From the summit of the rock the views are so singularly great and pleasing that they ought never to be omitted.'

Near the top of the climb, the quarry workings that produced all that scree become more evident, and *it is very important to keep younger children under close control here.*

With care, return to the main path below and turn right, heading downhill into the confines of Low Hows Wood. After a gate into the woodland, a narrow footbridge crosses a minor stream that soon joins forces with the River Derwent below. As the river is reached,

The Northern Fells from Castle Crag

turn right onto a signposted path for Rosthwaite **C**.

Now heading back to Seatoller, the continuing path wanders unhurriedly through delightful woodland, now close by the river, now moving farther away, but never in doubt.

Shortly after turning left at a signpost (still heading for Rosthwaite), an old quarry is encountered on the right, its remains producing an interesting, if rather wet, cave – a tentative peek from a distance is in order, but *closer exploration best avoided, especially by over-inquisitive children.*

Eventually the path breaks free of the woodland, and follows an easy route to a neat single-arch bridge (New Bridge **D**). Do not cross the bridge, but continue riverside, shortly passing a ford. A short section, heavily tree-rooted, preludes the rise of the path onto the top of a flood embankment, where the going is much easier.

Just after a farm, turn right into the grounds of Borrowdale Youth Hostel. Walk in front of the hostel, and onto a riverside path once more. This path seems to lead to an impasse – a rocky shoulder that

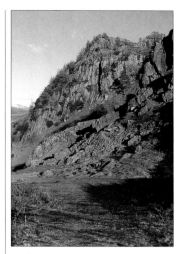

Castle Crag

comes down to meet the river apparently bars progress. Passage is assisted across the first part of this by chains fixed into the rock.

Once across, the path seems to disappear. Not instantly obvious, because a fence appears to block the onward route, the path has actually turned abruptly around the base of a low cliff to a narrow gate.

A good path now leads steadily on and eventually rises to meet a gate through a wall. Turn left and follow a clear path to another gate on the left giving into the car park at Seatoller. ●

Further Information

Safety on the Hills

The hills, mountains and moorlands of Britain, though of modest height compared with those in many other countries, need to be treated with respect. Friendly and inviting in good weather, they can quickly be transformed into wet, misty, windswept and potentially dangerous areas of wilderness in bad weather. Even on an outwardly fine and settled summer day, conditions can rapidly deteriorate. In winter, of course, the weather can be even more erratic and the hours of daylight are much shorter.

Therefore it is always advisable to take both warm and waterproof clothing, sufficient nourishing food, a hot drink, first-aid kit, torch and whistle. Wear suitable footwear such as strong walking boots or shoes that give a good grip over rocky terrain and on slippery slopes. Try to obtain a local weather forecast and bear it in mind before you start. Do not be afraid to abandon your proposed route and return to your starting point in the event of a sudden and unexpected deterioration in the weather. Do not go alone. Allow enough time to finish the walk well before nightfall.

Tarn Hows

Most of the walks described in this book do not venture into remote wilderness areas and will be safe to do, given due care and respect, at any time of year in all but the most unreasonable weather. Indeed, a crisp, fine winter day often provides perfect walking conditions, with firm ground

Steel End from Braithwaite Lodge, Newlands Valley

underfoot and a clarity that is not possible to achieve in the other seasons of the year. A few walks, however, are suitable only for reasonably fit and experienced hill walkers able to use a compass and should definitely not be tackled by anyone else during the winter months or in bad weather, especially high winds and mist. These are indicated in the general description that precedes each of the walks.

Global Positioning System (GPS)

What is GPS?

Global Positioning System, or GPS for short, is a fully-functional navigation system that uses a network of satellites to calculate positions, which are then transmitted to hand-held receivers.

By measuring the time it takes a signal to reach the receiver, the distance from the satellite can be estimated. Repeat this with several satellites and the receiver can then triangulate its position, in effect telling the receiver exactly where you are, in any weather, day or night, anywhere on Earth.

GPS information, in the form of grid reference data, is increasingly being used in Jarrold guidebooks, and many readers find the positional accuracy GPS affords a reassurance, although its greatest benefit comes when you are walking in remote, open countryside or through forests.

GPS has become a vital global utility, indispensable for modern navigation on land, sea and air

Cat Bells reflected in Derwent Water

around the world, as well as an important tool for map-making and land surveying.

Follow the Country Code
- Be safe – plan ahead and follow any signs
- Leave gates and property as you find them
- Protect plants and animals, and take your litter home
- Keep dogs under close control
- Consider other people

(Natural England)

Useful Organisations

Council for National Parks
6-7 Barnard Mews,
London
SW11 1QU
Tel. 020 7924 4077
www.cnp.org.uk

Campaign to Protect Rural England
128 Southwark Street,
London SE1 0SW
Tel. 020 798 12800
www.cpre.org.uk

Cumbria Tourism
Ashleigh, Holly Road,
Windermere, Cumbria
LA23 2AQ
Tel. 01539 822 222
www.golakes.co.uk

Cumbria Wildlife Trust
Plumgarths, Crook Road,
Kendal LA8 8LX
Tel. 01539 816300
www.wildlifetrust.org.uk/cumbria

English Heritage
PO Box 569, Swindon SN2 2YP
Tel. 0870 333 1181
www.english-heritage.org.uk

Forestry Commission
Lakes Forest District,
Grizedale, Hawkshead,
Ambleside,
Cumbria LA22 0QJ
Tel. 01229 860373

Friends of the Lake District
Murley Moss, Oxenholme Road,
Kendal, Cumbria LA9 7SS
Tel. 01539 720788
www.fld.org.uk

Lake District National Park Authority
Murley Moss, Oxenholme Road, Kendal, Cumbria LA9 7RL
Tel. 01539 724555
www.lake-district.gov.uk.

National Park information centres (*not open all year):
*Bowness Bay: Glebe Road
01539 442895
Keswick: Moot Hall
01768 772645
*Ullswater: Glenridding
01768 482414

Lake District Visitor Centre
Brockhole, Windermere, Cumbria LA23 1LJ
Tel. 015394 46601

National Trust (Borrowdale)
The Hollens, Grasmere, Ambleside, Cumbria LA22 9QZ
Tel. 01539 435599
Grasmere Information Centre and Shop,
Tel. 015394 35245

Natural England
Northminster House, Peterborough PE1 1UA
Tel. 0845 600 3078
www.naturalengland.org.uk

Ordnance Survey
Romsey Road, Maybush, Southampton SO16 4GU
Tel. 08456 05 05 05
www.ordnancesurvey.co.uk

The Ramblers' Association
2nd Floor, Camelford House, 87–90 Albert Embankment, London SE1 7TW
Tel. 020 7339 8500
www.ramblers.org.uk

Traveline (bus information):
0871 200 2233

Weathercall
www.weatherline.co.uk

Youth Hostels Association
Trevelyan House, Dimple Road, Matlock, Derbyshire DE4 3YH.
Tel. 01629 592600
www.yha.org.uk
For Lake District bookings contact:
Tel. 0870 770 6113

Ordnance Survey Maps of the Lake District
Explorer maps:
OL4 – The English Lakes – North Western area
OL5 – The English Lakes – North Eastern area
OL6 – The English Lakes – South Western area
OL7 – The English Lakes – South Eastern area

Answers to Questions

Walk 1: A schoolroom

Walk 2: A field guide will help you to identify them, but you should keep an eye open for warblers like chiffchaff, willow warbler and whitethroat, pied flycatchers, redstart and in spring cuckoos, as well as the more commonplace blackbirds and thrushes.

Walk 3: No, it was man-made by damming the outflow of a much smaller lake.

Walk 4: Because it was for the common use of all the villagers, mainly for grazing animals.

Walk 5: Get a leaflet from the visitor centre, and see how many you can identify.

Walk 6: The Brathay.

Walk 8: No height recorded but estimate is about 15ft (5m).

Walk 9: Check the view indicator to see how many you got right.

Walk 10: It is from the lake by the dairy pastures, a place where butter was made.

Walk 11: Wordsworth's daughter.

Walk 12: Patterdale.

Walk 13: Bluebell.

Walk 14: Have a look on the information panels and find out.

Walk 15: Have a look at your map and find out. (Maiden Moor and High Spy.)

Walk 16: The Coniston Fells.

Walk 17: Maple.

Walk 18: They are 'dovecotes' to allow doves and pigeons to get in and out.

Walk 19: It ran from Penrith via Keswick to Cockermouth.

Walk 20: Sir William Hamer and his family in memory of his son John.